T0157903

Secrets of the Heart

Poetry that explains what we are truly feeling

Michael Vincent Dlask

iUniverse, Inc.
New York   Bloomington

Secrets of the Heart
Poetry that explains what we are truly feeling

iUniverse books may be ordered through booksellers or by contacting:

*iUniverse
1663 Liberty Drive
Bloomington, IN 47403
www.iuniverse.com
1-800-Authors (1-800-288-4677)*

*Because of the dynamic nature of the Internet, any Web addresses or links
contained in this book may have changed since publication and may no longer be
valid.*

ISBN: 978-1-4502-3745-1 (sc)
ISBN: 978-1-4502-3746-8 (ebk)

Printed in the United States of America

iUniverse rev. date: 4/25/2011

Contents

Alone

Take away all the fame and fortune and what do you have left
You think they are the only things that you need to be happy
When in fact you don't need any of the above
The best things might be hidden but they are well kept
If you look hard enough you won't be able to see
Instead of being pulled closer you would rather shove
Losing everything isn't the worst of anything
Unless you didn't have a thing in the world to lose
Many people like to write and most love to sing
While the rest rather forget and go straight to the booze
You should think long and hard and believe in your heart
And treasure the things that are most important to you
It might be nothing to others but it's all you got
Knowing that you won't ever change and are not about to start
Faking your ways is the only thing that you can't do
Trying to be something that you wish you were not
Don't be the person to be waiting for the ringing of the phone
Because as long as you have something you will never be alone

Anger

Something you can control, most of the time, but not always
That's why I learned at a young age to occupy my mind
If you think of other things instead of hurting yourself
You'll find out that it's not worth getting upset about
And the more anger you acquire, the less you can get rid of it
Ripping your insides, making you suffer for many days
Knowing that soon, your soul is what you must find
So remove your books and put that anger back on the shelf
It's better there than with you, no matter the amount
Even though we all have it, it's something we won't admit
Can't ask for help, if we're used to doing it independently
So we torture many different and difficult things
Not knowing how much pain we really were going through
Pulling our lives closer and closer to the limitations of danger
Thinking that flames was the only thing we could see
Learning why we can't express our true feelings
Making us feel like we didn't even know what to do
So we should think before we release our anger

Beneath

Many people think that they can tell a person just by the way they look
Making you wonder how it is possible, if they can't see what's inside
Sure they can be tough on the outside, but what if it's a disguise
Never assume the expected, always prepare for the unusual
Because if you are, then there won't be any hidden surprises
Unless they are so clever to escape your mysterious suspicions
So instead of being quick to the draw, learn to get to know them
Because you'll never know, what lies beneath their heart
Whatever it might be, you wouldn't be able to find it in any book
In fact you shouldn't be shocked or amazed, if they commit suicide
Realizing that rumors do hurt, no matter if they are just lies
Wondering why can't things just go back to normal
Feeling the same way about everything, knowing that you can't be bias
Thinking it over in your head, coming up with the right solutions
Letting everyone know exactly where you stand or come from
Understanding that you're more than a work of art
Looking beyond the soul, to discover what is kept very deep
Hoping that nobody knew, that you talk in your sleep

Blind

Just because you're blind doesn't mean you can't see
You don't see with your eyes, but with your heart
Knowing that everything is equal and left in total darkness
Being pushed into someone you would rather not be
Throwing your trust and honor up in the air, ripping it apart
Realizing that nobody cared and your deaths last kiss
Sure pain has no effect on you since you're accustomed to the suffering
But pain doesn't always come from a whip, it comes from within
If you can't see it, doesn't mean it's not real
Treating you like a cripple, forgetting that you're a human being
Ashamed of knowing you, locking you up in some kind of storage bin
Not asking, but assuming that you are unable to feel
Forgetting that you lost the world not the other way around
Remembering that the smiles and laughter ended a long time ago
Listening to all the voices that ever made a sound
Not knowing if it's your friend or just another foe
So don't be upset if my will or last testament ain't signed
Because I didn't die stupid just a little bit blind

Change

People think that with some help, they are able to change
Not just for themselves, but for you as well
Forgetting that no matter what, you'll change if you want to
Sure you could change your appearance and attitude
But can you change who you are what you have become
Thinking that you'll reach them knowing their out of range
Trying to trap you with their lies, as they begin to sell
Pouring out everything exactly the way you ever knew
Knowing that they're not listening, making them act very rude
Ending up just like the rest, alone and lonesome
So if you believe in your heart, then you'll make the right
Unaware that through this process, you are changing rapidly
Not by choice, but mere conscience and something forced upon
Realizing the nature of this improvement and are very grateful
Remembering that you can't change your dreams, because it's
your passion
And even though you might not be focused, it's all you can see
Looking for a way to get to you by using your only son
Getting you confused with another, knowing that your life will
be wonderful

Competition

Even though this is fun, doesn't mean it's not a competition
No matter how much you give, it's not enough to beat me
I'm the best there was and ever will be
I was given this special talent to teach and enlighten you
Sure you have seen many styles, but none quite like mine
Learning new and amazing ways as I complete my dictation
Explaining how there is more to life than a simple late fee
Looking deep within knowing that it's the key
The key to success of to failure really depends on what you do
Don't worry, I have faith and think you will do just fine
If not, at least you did the best you could
Thinking that you were way ahead, while I was nowhere in sight
When in reality, I was right in front undetected
Not surprised that every time we had a contest, like you knew I would
Realizing that I'm known for my intelligence and not my height
Just because you can't seem to beat me, isn't what you expected
Doesn't allow you to think that you need my permission
So give it up, because with me, there is no competition

Deep

My poems might be complex, but I'm not a normal person
Just, because I take them deep, from within my heart
Doesn't mean that I can't try to explain my true life
Having to take down all the walls, which was well buried
Made it even harder, knowing that it was hidden on purpose
Trying to keep my mouth closed and shove it way under my skin
Knowing exactly how to finish, with no idea on how to start
So close your eyes take a deep breath and grasp it with a knife
Sure it can be very painful, but remember, it's not that scary
It is something you would rather forget and hardly will ever miss
Knowing that once told, it tends to take the pressure off
Wondering why it was hurting, more than the original saga
Not aware of how many times it has twisted and turned
Keeping you awake for several years, not allowing you to sleep
Hoping to get it out of your system, through a simple cough
Feeling like you're as empty as a desert and out of aqua
Treating everyone with respect, while getting used to being burned
Realizing that it takes a tough and patient person to dig that deep

Destiny

It isn't just your fate, it's your destiny
Determining if it's a choice that you are willing to make
Is all up to you no matter if you are blind or able to see
If pain and suffering is something you can handle then you won't break
Sacrificing all you have isn't anything you want to encounter
But at many times you have no choice and have to like it
Thinking that you will be prepared for the next time it shall occur
Knowing that you have the power to change is the only thing you will admit
Don't let others tell or control your ways of thinking
Unless you are ready for disappointment and punishment
Because if not cautious it would be done without blinking
And there will not be any remorse once it is sent
Believing in yourself may be the only way you'll ever succeed
So reach high in the sky and exceed your limitations
No matter what others say, you will be what you want to be
Realizing if done right, it will be the last and only deed
Remembering that nothing can stop it as long as it's your own expectations
Trusting that you have chosen to fulfill your destiny

Erase

If you could erase all the bad things, then you would
Knowing that you can't only makes you more mad
Not at all the world, for the simple fact that it can't be changed
Forgetting that you did your best and all that you could
Clearing all your thoughts and ideas that you ever had
Watching it begin to turn bright into dark as it faded
Feeling guilty in many different ways, thinking that you should
Realizing it was your fault that everything went bad
Trying to fix it before you got yourself erased
Running out of time, looking for some kind of relief
Wondering why it was taking too long to figure out
Giving everything up because you weren't left anything
Not caring if it took your life, as long as others were spared
Sure sacrifice was everything you believed to be against
But it was something you couldn't begin to count
Not because of what you did, but of your constant lying
Being feared instead of getting the respect that you wanted
Learning that correcting them will only make a mence

Fall

No matter how many times you get to the top, you will fall
Now how you decide to get back up will be all up to you
You can take the dive, or just do it with grace and determination
If you choose right, you will get up, dust yourself off and do it again
This time you have nothing that can hold you any lower than you are
Knowing that you have a lot of experience on your side
Patience might not be something you want, but it's what you need
Learning how to use it, will enable you to avoid getting pushed into the wall
Not giving a second thought, knowing that it is what you have to do
Doing things that are impossible for you to even imagine
Telling yourself to keep focus, and stick with the original plan
Realizing that this feeling is what's going to get you very far
It might be dangerous, but you are willing to take this ride
Being a follower, when you are meant and suppose to lead
Will only make your mouth water, and harder on your lips
Don't wait to be told what to do and don't expect a call
Because the greatest things in the world are under our fingertips
And all we have to do, is catch them before we fall

Fear

Fear is more of an emotion, than it is a feeling
It is something you can see and touch
Knowing that the results are either painful or unbearable
Understanding the knowledge and fact of this emotion
Wondering if it can be stopped and placed under our control
Anticipating every move and thought, that it might bring
Not knowing if denial was preventing you from hurting so much
Realizing that this isn't a fantasy turning into a fable
It is simply the hard work of your deepest dedication
Taking many things away, leaving you with only your soul
Thinking of the only way to get rid of this fear
Is to fight it head on and hope for little cost
No matter if you have to give up your life to get it
Remembering that you weren't just frightened, but scared
Hurting from the sorrow of the people who didn't care
Treating you not as their own, but as you were lost
Pushing and throwing you into the bottom of their pit
For this was the worst that you have ever feared

Fiction

Just because something is said, it doesn't mean it's real
A lot of people get the facts confused with the actual truth
Thinking that there is no difference between that and fiction
Coming to realize that if dreamt, than it might be possible
But don't get your hopes up, if you think it's going to come to
you
Because if you want it bad enough, you will do what you need
to fulfill
Making things fall in place unaware that it would be this nice
and smooth
Knowing that this isn't just an adrenaline, it's an addiction
Forgetting your limits, not aware that you are capable
Remembering that no matter what, you are responsible for
whatever you do
Sure you can pretend you live in a wonderful and exciting world
Keeping this lie for several weeks or months, is my prediction
Because it is hard to control fantasy over any kind of reality
Some people like to get you around their fingers and twirl
Believing that you are stupid, because you don't have their
education
When you rather use your heart to feel and not see
Taking in all the pressures and disasters without regret
Hoping that the day will come, when this will eventually offset

Fight

When I was young, I used to love to fight
Not with my hands, but with my head
Even though I didn't know much back then, I would argue
If I only knew, the stuff I know now
Then I would of realized how stupid I really was
Locked in a room, instead of having fun flying a kite
Sitting in the dark, until it was time to go to bed
Scared and frightened because I didn't understand what was true
No matter how badly I was hurt, I couldn't say ow
Knowing that if I did, they would have just cause
Inflicting pain on and around me, is all they ever cared about
Hoping that I wouldn't have a chance to tell the tale
I could tell you that I had a great life, but I'm not a liar
Being woken up and beaten, for nothing almost every night
Having dried eyes, because I couldn't even pout
Many thought I was a ghost, because I became very pale
Not knowing why, I loved and enjoyed playing with fire
Now I do anything I can, to avoid getting into any kind of a fight

Guess

You think that just one look at me, you can guess who I am
What I've been through and exactly how I react to things
Well you can't, because it's the inside that counts, not the outer
So, if you want to judge someone before you know them
Then stop wasting your time on me, and spend it on those who care
Because my heart only talks to those who listen, without building a dam
As long as you learn the truth, you won't hurt my feelings
Even though I'm nice and sweet, I'm nothing that you'll prefer
Knowing that you rather be lied to, forgetting what you have become
Living your life in total chaos with nothing to fear
Trying to guess or figure out why I'm one of a kind
Realizing that unlike others, I do have a conscience
And do whatever I have to make my heart right
Sure people say many things to make me look like a mess
But, if you are as smart, you'll be happy with what you will find
Believing that with me, you won't have to ever be cautious
Wishing that you can hold and hang onto me throughout the night
So next time you see me, you wouldn't have to guess

Hope

Hope can be a good thing, only when used properly
Most of the time, it is used to relieve a lot of our stress
When some of the time, we don't even expect it
If you need or want it, you wouldn't have a clue
Doing all you have to do, believing in true honesty
You only feel bad if you lied and had to confess
Being helped is something you would rather not admit
Because hope to you is something you made up or drew
Not knowing the reaction, it will perceive of many people
Trying to erase the memories that this has portrayed
Knowing that if not done, there will be trouble
Wishing that you wouldn't have to experience anything like this
But as we know, most of the time we don't have any control
And even if we did, containing it, we wouldn't be able
Because who ever said dreams don't come true, lied
Or was one who liked to be a follower and go with the flow
Messing with disaster, waiting for death's last kiss
When hope is the only thing left for us to keep our soul

Hurt

Sure we hurt many people in a lot of different ways
But are we for certain that it was planned or on purpose
And if they don't say a word, how would we know
Making us feel sorrow for no reason, losing many days
Knowing that we didn't cause any of this
Expecting us to take this lying down and go with the flow
Letting them walk all over us like we were nothing
Because we are too sincere and in love with them
Well all that has to stop, so the pain can be restored
So if the pain is gone, then we won't hurt no more
Wrong if you think that, because we are hurt even without it
We are hurt, when we see all of our friends dying
It might scare most, but it will definitely effect some
Seeing them shot in the back would have been better than being
fried
Realizing that we have been down this road before
Getting beaten anywhere we chose to sit
In a secluded area letting all your anger out
Believing that in this world we actually do count

Identity

A card doesn't tell us who we are, or where we come from
We define that by the character, we have obtained
Knowing that building it might, and will take your life
Being humble is nothing we ask for or expect
Sure you always try to be nice and sweet helping others
Putting yourself last, forgetting that you wrote this poem
Floating down some river wasn't anything, you ever wanted
But at least you won't be remembered as the one with the knife
Even though you didn't like someone you gave them respect
Some identify you not as a human, but by their colors
Just because a person is difficult to understand
Don't give up on them, for you may be their last resort
Being mean is the only way they know how to express
themselves
Hurting inside is something they wouldn't want to tell you
And having you not say a word, is what they will demand
Knowing that it will hold up in the highest court
Thinking that their presence, brought us a lot of happiness
So our identity is a secret, that you know to be true

Integrity

Stop letting your pride and honor get the best of you
Just because you think that your road is the only one traveled
Doesn't mean that you have to give up, if you don't get your way
Earning their respect is one thing you have to learn to receive
Forgetting everything that you ever knew just to save your integrity
Maybe this is the life that you were intended to lead
Unlike other things, you have no choice in this situation
Finding a piece to complete this puzzle is harder without a single clue
Remembering that there wasn't a thing left untouched
So before you talk, please think of what you might say
Because when it spreads, you won't know what to believe
Don't think that if you open your eyes, you'll be able to see
When you rather stick with the plans of your creed
Knowing that it will be the last resort of any solution
Taking back the blame to bring the honor to the place it belongs
Wondering if it was worth everything, that you told me
Trying to understand why you have to use different types of tongues
Accepting this challenge, knowing that it won't be pretty

Jewel

She is as sweet as a peach, and precious as a jewel
This is a taste that you can't and won't want to forget
Her hair is nice and soft making your fingers feel like gold
Looking through her beautiful eyes, so you can see them sparkle
Knowing that with her, everything just seems to fit
Placing all the cards on the table not ever going to be told
Being energized because she gives you a lot of fuel
Loving to listen to every word is something you like to admit
Thinking that it wouldn't be possible if it wasn't told
Asking yourself if this girl is for real, or just a fairy tale
Hoping not to ever find out because she is the perfect one for you
Making you feel like you have a reason to come home
Showing you that by being yourself, you can be happy
Going to the park, having fun playing with her on the leaves
Enjoying every minute, knowing that this was true
Sure you have many words, but you can't compare her to a poem
You have to believe your heart, so you can see
That she is very special, and will always be your jewel

Journey

A journey is an adventure that tends to change
You never know if luck is going to be on your side or not
So without any worries, you begin to plan your trip
Not aware if you're missing something or just too excited
Just want to get away and out of people's range
Going to a place that is neither cold nor is it hot
Taking life by the throat with a nice firm grip
Trying to understand what exactly makes us feel like we are
united
Learning many mysteries of our land from past to present
Amazed of how well the pilots know precisely where they have
to go
Sure there is many highways and streets that are connected
But who really knows if they are a help or an extreme danger
I guess you have to take the negative with the positive
Driving across the country to know what the landmarks actually
meant
Soaking in all the knowledge of the greatest teachers you will
ever know
They might not be around anymore, but they really got things
started
So it all depends on what you want or what you rather prefer
Wherever your journey takes you, at least it is great to be alive

Kind Hearted

The less you give the least is expected or acquired from you
But the more you provide, the more they will take
You might resist at first, but your heart makes you give
Trying to stop it, but it is beyond your control
Being kind hearted is something everyone knows to be true
Taking advantage of every mistake that you always seem to make
Knowing that being nice and sweet is the only way you'll ever live
Waiting to see what it takes to get you to forget and just blow
Forgetting that you ain't what you used to be when you were young
Learning how to manage your anger instead of igniting it
Making them mad because you beat them to their own punch line
Realizing that even though it hurts, it also destroys them worst
Wondering if you are this way to feel like you actually belong
Or was it because you didn't care, not even a bit
It doesn't matter whatever it was as long as you are fine
Hoping that you won't cry even if you explode or burst
So even if your kind hearted doesn't mean you can't be rejected
Because the harder you try the easier you will get denied

Limit

There is just so much you can take without giving in
Being forced or pushed to and beyond your limit
Knowing that they stepped over the line, and need to be punished
But you know that silence damaged them the worst
Since punishing them wasn't your style or intention
No matter how much the ice would become thin
Even if you have high limits, it's something you won't admit
Not what others put on you, but what you are required
Doing whatever you can, so you will be the first
Realizing the possibility of fulfilling your destination
Don't let anyone set or rule how much your goal should be
Because if you want to succeed, there is no set goal
Learning that if you let them get their way, you will be average
Convinced that you didn't want any of this
Working hard pass your limitations to get to your destiny
Sacrificing everything you had, other than your soul
Leaving all your rage and anger locked up in a cage
Remembering the hard times, will be something you won't miss

Luck

They say without bad luck, we wouldn't have any at all
I believe that with special skills and talent you don't need it
Of course many great things can happen all in a row
But it was pure coincidence and has nothing to do with luck
If you needed luck, than you would of used a four leaf clover
Knowing that you don't want any part of it, you just make things happen
Hoping that your decisions will help you make the right call
Realizing that the knowledge you have learned, didn't come from any kit
It came from your heart, and that's all you know
Since you refused luck in your corner, watch your back
Because luck is very tricky, it will either get you or your lover
So, if you want to be safe, then don't leave yourself open
Now that we have it under control, things will be back to normal
Wondering if luck really exists or is it just a reason
Why do they rather depend on it, instead of admitting their mistakes
Being yourself is better than someone who acts too formal
Not worrying about what others think, even if they get the wrong perceptions
But know that it's not over, because luck will do whatever it takes

Madison

I thought after losing Kaitlyn, I wouldn't have any love left
But you proven me wrong, by your big beautiful blue eyes
Giving a smile, so bright it shined up the whole room
Seeing you for the first time was not only amazing, but enlightening
Learning many different and unique things from your growth
Teaching me all the stuff that I forgot ever existed
Being so innocent at heart, whenever you even slept
Trying to count and touch all the stars in the skies
Wondering what makes the flowers able to develop or blossom
Playing with your karaoke machine, because you love to sing
Making lots of noise, just like you did at your birth
Having fun and enjoying your toys, is all that you ever wanted
Knowing your abc's and having the ability to count to ten
Can't wait for the school year to come through this summer
Loving to walk, skip and jump when others wanted you to run
Drawing pictures with crayons and markers, having no interest in a pen
Hoping that you'll never forget me, when you get older
Because I'll always remember what makes you my sweet Madison

Masterpiece

Even though this is my masterpiece, it will be the last
I enjoyed every minute, that I had spent with you
Thanks for listening to my problems and giving me solutions
You won't begin to understand how grateful I am
I would tell, but I don't have that much time left
Wondering why everything you love, goes so fast
Taking all the pain and suffering, is all that I ever knew
Not knowing what's going on, brings me to many conclusions
Closing all the doors, only to hear the slam
Knowing that in my heart, is where my key to success is kept
Realizing it wasn't anything, but poetry, that held me together
Sure I had plenty of lovers in and out of my life
But it didn't keep me alive, it liked to torture me
Learning that it didn't mean a thing, because I'm used to worst
If you think I'm a fighter, your wrong, I am a lover
That's why it was easy for me to give up my wife
Forgetting that I used my heart and not my eyes to see
Being last to say goodbye, but at the gates, I will be first

Mirror

You don't have to account to nobody, but the person in the
mirror
Sure you can lie, cheat and steal your way in life
But its not worth selling yourself short or losing your soul
Because the more you do it, the less chance you have getting out
So live your life the way you expect to be treated
Not what others have done to you in past and present
Show them how genuine you really are and how much you do
care
Learning that you are straight forward and sharp as a knife
Instead of pushing your weight, you rather pull
Doing things by yourself is what you are all about
Not conceited or controlling, but exactly what you have
demanded
When many thought that you were selfish, just because you very
independent
Realizing that there was more to this book than the cover
Amazed of how wrong they were, when you proved them
different
Not knowing if you would be serious or sincere
What ever you decided was the choice they had to prefer
Because if you followed your heart, you will be at least decent
Then you wouldn't have to worry about that cracked mirror

Mistake

We all make them, whether or not it's good or bad
Some people spend their whole lives trying to figure it out
If it was a mistake or just a disaster waiting to happen
Either way you make it, learn from it, and move on to the next
Can't dwell in the past thinking of the first mistake
Even though there was nothing you could do or say about it
Knowing that a mistake is like playing dominoes
When one goes down, the rest begins to follow the pattern
Sometimes we create mistakes to make other people mad
And don't care if they begin to cry or even pout
It might be mean, but at least our minds are what we open
Realizing that no matter what had happened we tried our best
Cleaning all the garbage that we seldom make
Not having enough time to realize that the fire wasn't even lit
Most of the time, mistakes are made because nobody really knows
Of course they'll admit it because it's their turn
Mistakes are made all the time, but we tend to forget
The ones that we seem to remember are what we'll always regret

Normal

You think I'm normal, when in reality I'm not
Sure many had tough and terrifying lives, but none like mine
Even though you were locked in a room, you weren't forgotten
Might of got beaten, but at least you were loved
I wish, it was that easy and clear for me
But nothing works the way you expect or anticipate
For me, they didn't forget, they just chose not to care
Being alone was my only comfort, receiving satisfaction in what
I got
Knowing that unlike most, I am one of a kind
Trying to forget, but remembering that things do happen
Sometimes for no reason, even though you are shoved
Learning that it might seem dark, but you will be able to see
And find out that it only takes you, to seal your fate
You can blame the whole world, and think it's not fair
Or you can decide to take a stand for your dedication
Putting together everything, that came from your heart and
soul
Doing what is right for yourself, should be your only occupation
Because no one can truly define what is not normal

Notice

Notice might be a simple word, but it's all you ask
Even though they don't care or appreciate the things you've done
So just because they're selfish doesn't give them the right to judge
Treating them, with respect is the only thing you did wrong
Taking all their grief and laziness became your daily task
Wondering why your heart left and your mind was all alone
Knowing that you gave it up each and every night at the local lodge
Placing a rock in front of you, making you feel like you don't belong
Realizing that if they wanted to notice, then they would
It's their loss not yours, so don't you forget that
They might later down the road, ask for another chance
Hoping that you somehow find it in your heart to forgive
When in fact, you wouldn't waste your time, even if you could
Because unlike them, you would be able to smell a rat
Not prejudging them just because you want them in your pants
But because your you and it's the best you can give
You shouldn't allow anyone to just step all over you
Remembering that even though your unique, you are also true

Omen

You are born into a world, when the possibilities are endless
But, what most countries don't know, is that their omen is planned
Luckily for you, you live in a place where you control your destiny
It's not decided, unless you want or make it possible
You might have an idea, but don't believe it is a good one
So you destroy or crush it, without knowing it's omen
If I was you, I would learn to trust my instincts
Sure you might be smart and intelligent in everything you do
But is it worth it, if you all of a sudden became clueless
And find out that your time was spent being trapped
Thinking that this can't be right, so how can this be
Well it can and will, no matter if you're critical or stable
Being punished for things you thought of and not what you've done
Throwing you through the window, leaving your body in the open
Not knowing or caring about you or your associated links
Creating a mess so bad, that they are stuck like glue
Closing all the doors, having no choice, but to let them in
Making them think, they have total control of your omen

Ordeal

You do a lot of things in your life, trying to make it better
But most of the time, it doesn't happen like that, does it
Being pushed into a situation, that you can't refuse or walk away
from
Making it more impossible to avoid this whole entire ordeal
Sure you can say that you don't want it, but you have no choice
No matter what you do, you're just making things worse than
before
Thinking that you have control, while the power belongs to
another
Knowing that success has nothing to do with climbing a ladder
Doing whatever it took for survival, is the only thing that you
see fit
Not aware of that special payday, looking for a one time sum
Taking any job you can, not caring on the way you feel
Just doing your work without complain, knowing you have no
voice
Getting out of line will only knock you straight to the floor
So if you're thinking about talking, don't even bother
They created this disaster, not for fun, but to teach you a lesson
This isn't something you can buy out of or even make a deal
Realizing that life is more than just thick and thin
Trying to understand why it happens, looking to give meaning
to this ordeal

Passion

You might enjoy poetry, but it's my only true passion
Sure many things come and go over the course of your lifetime
Knowing that poetry is the only thing that will last forever
Realizing with it, you shall receive a better perception
Not worrying if any of the information has to rhyme
Believing in yourself, not having to pull that special lever
Which includes the thought of reaching in your magic sack
Taking out words and phrases that nobody knew existed
Enjoying every single second of each and every task
Having too much fun, thinking of it more of an journey than a routine
Remembering that it is something you shall never lack
Helping everyone no matter if they are sick or twisted
Because unlike most people, you are unique and don't wear a mask
Amazed of how your heart is all that can be seen
Thinking more of the future, than the present
Trying to build yourself a clear and solid foundation
Making your word count, proving that you are what you meant
Learning that without a heart, you have no passion

Potion

You get three chances to mess up this potion
The first time can and will hurt, but they will forgive
And the second is an indication of a pattern, about to form
If you are smart, there won't be a third or you'll be no more
See with the right ingredients you can't go wrong
Working most of your life trying to succeed perfection
There is nothing that your heart won't be able to achieve
Knowing that too much of anything can cause a storm
Being tossed up in the air landing all over the floor
Feeling and not knowing that something just doesn't belong
So before you decide to judge, forget about it
Because would you like to be accused without knowing
Or classified as a group that you're not a part of
Don't care who you are, just worried about your occupation
Well, I didn't think so, not even a little bit
Only wanting to be trusted and not be pulled by a string
Not knowing the real meaning of true everlasting love
Hoping that within time someone will have your potion

Power

Power is the curse of your never ending love kept deep inside
Sure you can control many nations within your fingertips
But what good is it, if you can't keep your heart calm
Knowing that with this power, there will be consequences
Taking responsibility and action without a place to hide
Listening and obeying every word that comes from your lips
Realizing that you have them eating out of your palm
So it does have many advantages under different circumstances
But only the strongest shall surpass the limitations
Not in body or shape, but the one that's in order, your mind
Without it in total control, you will be lost forever
Wondering if you'll ever gain all the access that you require
Not knowing if you'll take what it wants to offer
Leaving everything we dream up to our imaginations
Believing that with this special power, great things you shall
find
Discovering the many differences of the magic is what you
prefer
Learning all that you can get your hands on or acquire
For this knowledge, you will be given all of the power

Quest

If you think you're going to beat me at my own game, good
luck
Because you will need it just to keep in step with me
I could be slow at times, but to the point and very precise
So if not careful or aware of my dedication, you will be stuck
Lost in a maze not knowing who or what you will see
Sure you'll find many ways and ideas to get the advice
But luck doesn't seem to comprehend with all your plans
It wants you to figure out the solution to this major problem
Knowing for a fact that there is no way you even have a prayer
Trying to meet the deadline regardless of the demands
Biting your nails constantly and swallowing your gum
Preparing yourself for the worst only makes things better
Focusing on that one thing that makes us truly happy
Realizing once complete then there will not be any looking back
If you want to follow your dreams, then I'll wish you the best
Just keep it up and don't think of losing that key
It is very precious and something most people lack
You might think this as an adventure, but it's your favorite quest

Quick

Just because you are quick, doesn't mean you're efficient
Being slow isn't a bad thing as long as you do the right thing
Knowing that the quicker you are, the more mistakes are made
Unless you have all the confidence that it takes for a daily routine
You will be lost, with no idea of what has to get done
Trying many new things, day in and day out, will only increase your skills
The more you are dedicated the quicker you will become
So in order to be fast, learn to be very patient and willing
See if you're not and do everything at once you will be sick
And if not cautious, then you would have more than an accident
Realizing that you are smart and clever, because you were actually listening
Not forgetting to take notes, knowing that it will start to fade
And even if you keep your eyes opened, it still won't be seen
Don't blink, because you won't even notice that it has been long gone
Finally learning that quickness, has nothing to do with taking energy pills
Sure you might find yourself in the dust, but at least you're not dumb
Doing the best you can, will always be your greatest feeling
Proving that as long as you are sharp, you won't have to be quick

Revival

For many years people have, declared my life as undesirable
Not knowing that this is the year that, it all changes
Sure death was always in your face, but you learned to accept it
Now you are stronger, than ever to announce your revival
Ready to enjoy life for the first time, despite what it has given you
Knowing that your past should be left, and your future should be right
Pushing yourself passed the limits, showing that you are capable
Loving every minute of it, treating everyone like they are famous
Making you happy to remember, that they once wrote kit
Aware that it meant, to keep in touch and not to lose your soul
Locking yourself in a room, that you had no idea of what to do
Being surrounded by darkness, trying to reach the light
Turning your life around, so you can savor every precious moment
Because you'll never know, how short it really can be
So taking this kind of approach will make your mind more opened
Letting you have the experience of the present
Giving you a world so complex, that you can actually see
Realizing that this revival, is the best thing that ever happened

Revolve

You think that if your sick or not around, the world stands still
Well it doesn't, because it revolves with or without you
No matter how much you fight it, you can't win
So don't believe that you can't make a difference
Because you can and will as long as you're devoted
Dedication is the main ingredient to expressing the way you will
feel
But the heart guides you to everything you have to do
Even though it might look like a moral sin
If things don't work out, don't give up and lose your patience
Knowing that whatever you do or say, you are being watched
Just because a door closes doesn't mean it can't revolve
And if a window is shut, then can it be opened
Saying no, only means that you have no idea what to think
Learning for a fact, that this puzzle is something you can't solve
Believing that it might have been shut, but was it locked
Not knowing, if you were alright or had too much to drink
Waking up, wondering if your actions were taken to heart
Realizing that it wasn't called for, and it was ripping you apart

Routine

We wake up, take a shower, and get ready for work
Without thinking, as part of our daily routine
Not even aware that we do this every night and day
Wondering if we will ever break it, or will it become us
Wishing, that someone would just pull the cork
Because it's driving you crazy, and making you go insane
Just because you're used to it, doesn't mean you have to obey
Knowing that there is no reason to even put up a fuss
Realizing that this is making you very predictable
And you don't like it one way or the other
So you try to change, but have no idea on how
Seeking advice from friends, knowing that they just got over it
Giving you many choices that you believe are unforgettable
Hoping that you listened to them, instead of her
Making your head hurt, to the point, you say ow
Changing your direction is the only way you see fit
So if you're having any problems, please come clean
Because we will be able to get out of this basic routine

Sustain

If something is lost or forgotten, than it doesn't even exist
Trying to sustain all the memories, that we have endured over
the years
Remembering the best of times, just to avoid the agony and
pain
Thinking that controlling it, is the only way to get rid of it
When in fact, you should allow it through your heart
Because the more you bring it up, the better it becomes alive
Unsure of what you think, knowing that it will be lost forever
Keeping an eye on all the loved ones, that you added to your list
Not wanting to see, but have to look at the mirrors
Hoping that it will all wash away in the rain
Taking your emotions to a place where you can't put up a fit
Wondering when exactly, are things going to begin to start
Getting frustrated on how you are supposed to survive
Creating new ways and ideas, that makes you very clever
Still unable to get those painful events, out of your mind
Forgetting that all the troubles, are what made you insane
So when you look closer, it won't be hard to find
And you shouldn't let it bother you, because it will be easier to
sustain

Swept

You can give them boxed chocolate and a dozen of roses
But it doesn't mean, that you will be appreciated or thanked
So instead of being common, why not be happy, being yourself
Taking those long walks down the beach, that you know you'll enjoy
Surprising them with a candle light dinner, is something you love to do
Trying to get to their heart with comfort, surpassing the stomach
It might be hard work, but at least, you swept them off their feet
So remember that a window will open, as soon as the door closes
Not giving you a chance, if you wanted to know if you're compatible or linked
Making you wonder, if you are really true to oneself
Getting into many situations, without the help of any decoy
Being too busy to experience, the full effects of being blue
Realizing that being praised, would have been better than that swift kick
Knowing that you're the luckiest person, anyone would like to meet
Wondering why the darkness took so long, to show the sweetness
Can't blame yourself for forgetting, that it was even kept
You might of felt it, but you thought it was something you wouldn't miss
Being grateful that your past has just been swept

Switch

The only way people would understand your pain, is to pull a switch
Not the kind that you can turn on or off, whenever you want too
But the one, that places others in your own foot steps
Walking a day in your shoes, seeing the stuff that you deal with regularly
Realizing that half the things they said about you, isn't true
As far as them lying to you, it is impossible and hard to catch
Feeling their heart, realizing that they were always true to you
Wondering why they see everything clear, instead of many colors
Seeing through your own eyes, that they were actually nice and friendly
Thinking that all this time, you were wrong not knowing what to do
Determining if they should apologize or make things better
Being more consistent with the way people really feel
Not judging them before, you have the chance to know them
So they give you the respect, that you have earned and deserved
Listening to you, during the whole ordeal and not after
Knowing that you can be trusted, because you are for real
Learning that just because you can't impress everyone, you will some
Being calm makes this switch, nice and smooth, relaxing the main nerve

The Rise

There is a time that we have no choice, but to fall down
Without this fall, there is no need to make a great rise
Challenges shouldn't bring us down, it should just enlighten us
So we can learn our mistakes, as we proceed to move forward
Knowing that we have to continue our success, even if no one is
around
Remembering the knowledge of the people, who are truly wise
Realizing that it isn't worth your time or effort to fuss
Taking advantage of every opportunity to receive that special
award
Being kicked to the ground, is something you rather not prefer
Just because you spent most of your time in the dark room
Intrigued by not only mysterious things, but by the magic inside
them
Wondering if everyone was the same, then no one would ever
have fun
Because the world would be perfect with nobody to advise
And there wouldn't be a thing, for any one of us to offer
Wishing that we could listen, instead of being quick to assume
Not thinking that it was possible, to be this dumb
Deciding that you rather walk through the steps, then run
Gracefully waiting for the day, that you will rise

Transparent

Some say that I have a face that is impossible to forget
Remembering my unique ways of showing my love for everyone
But I'm not as transparent, as most people think I have become
You think, if they knew my real life, they would treat me the same
I believe that they won't be able to take the facts to be true
Because to me, they are better off if we never even met
Can't change the past or history, once something has been done
Knowing that what I did was wrong, but it wasn't dumb
So I messed up my legacy, but I am very proud of what I have became
Realizing that it is the best thing to happen to me, other than you
Despite the odds, that were destined for me, I disobeyed
Didn't care about the pain or suffering, that I have endured over the years
Not caring whether or not, I was going to live or die
Hoping that I was more appreciative to others than I was to myself
Sure there is nothing left for me, since I have been betrayed
Not by the common things, but by my beliefs of well known fears
Believing them is something that I never dared to try
Acting all scared, knowing it couldn't be all that tough

Trapped

You wish you could say something, but you can't
Because if you do, you have nowhere to go
Finding yourself lost in a world of misery and agony
Knowing that you are trapped by more hatred
Listening to the controlling hand, instead of your pure heart
Not caring if your soul was gone, as long as others were happy
No matter if they used or treated you like a door mat
Believing that you're not a person, who has any feelings
But someone who doesn't deserve to breathe the air
Deciding if it was something you wanted to grant
Considering that it was the only thing you didn't know
Asking yourself over and over, if you want to be
Knowing that it doesn't matter if you're alive or dead
Sure it would of made more sense, if told from the start
But separation is the only thing, I was allowed to see
And it was a place I don't remember, if I stood or sat
Now I wonder what ever happened to the little things
Because, they helped get rid of my one and only fear

Treasure

Your garbage can and will become someone else's treasure
It might not mean much to you, but it's everything to them
Sure you grew up with a silver spoon stuck in your mouth
When I had to work and scrape, just to survive
Knowing that I'm not the only one, who can think for
themselves
Learning that things become more sacred, as we begin to
mature
Doing everything that you can, even though it was dumb
Giving it all you got, so you shall have peace on earth
Realizing that being independent makes you feel more alive
At least, we can say that we done it by ourselves
If a box contains shredded paper, don't be mad or upset
You just have to be patient, and your treasure will arrive
It might not be what you were expecting, but it shall do
Because it's just the beginning of great things to come
Opening your treasure box, knowing that your life will be set
Even though it's not shining like jewelry, you will live
Having a feeling that your heart always knew
And it's not even close to what you may assume

True

If something is said, it doesn't mean it's true
Just because things seem to make sense and fall in place
Explaining in full detail, knowing for a fact it's not what I do
Remembering as far as evidence, there is no trace
Determining one way or another if its real is all up to you
It's not me, so please stay off my case
You could pour out your heart and they wouldn't have a clue
Wondering if all is done just so they can keep their face
But, if you hide behind your feelings then nobody would know
Making them wonder if you are serious or a plain fake
So tell them the truth and hope that they will understand
Because if not done, they will listen to the rumors and go with
the flow
Don't do this for me, but for your own sake
It's not that hard, just don't worry about where you will eventually
land
The truth might set you free, but it will also knock you down
Choosing your words carefully without making a sound
Realizing that the city ain't no different than a small town
Once the word gets out, there's no way to retrieve it
Trusting something no matter if it's true or make believe
No matter if the whole thing is made up or just a little bit
Wishing that it wouldn't be this difficult to achieve
Believing that they did everything in the world for you
Truth hurts so don't let it make you feel blue
Or you will forget what you thought you knew
Not knowing that being yourself is all that you had to do
Even though you don't think straight, your heart shall stay true

Unite

We tend to perceive many things as a normal way of living
Not aware of the opportunities that were passed down over the
years
Taking a strange and unusual tragedy to bring things back
together
Forgetting that we even exist, just to lend our hands to others
Trying to understand the true meaning of our existence
Being recognized as heroes, when all you did was your
occupation
Saving one person's life to you was worth losing your own
Putting on to the side, all the differences you might have had
Knowing that this day, you will have to fight
Hearing the nation through the skies, as it begins to sing
Bringing the emotions down to an arrangement of tears
Wondering if it was possible for these events to occur
Faced with the loss of their brothers and sisters
Getting ready for whatever it takes, keeping your patience
Fighting for your freedom, due to the current occasion
When loved ones are trying, to reach their cell phone
Looking to describe this day, making everybody so sad
Learning that we will prevail, as soon as we begin to unite

Vanish

You might of seen me yesterday or today, but you won't see me
tomorrow
Taking things day to day knowing that I have at least one left
Cherishing everything that I have, working to get what I want
Sure it will take a long time, but at least, I won't hurt no more
You or anyone else wouldn't even notice, when I decide to
vanish
Just for the fact, that you don't want to realize that I am alive
If it isn't for a favor, you tend to forget that I do exist
It's not your fault for thinking, that I go with the flow
Thinking that I wasn't listening, treating me like I was deaf
Wondering why I'm unique, and that there is no need to change
the font
Knowing that no matter what happens, I'm not going back to
before
Making my heart stronger than ever, realizing that I am rich
Going to my old ways, not worried if I will ever survive
I don't care if I'm at the bottom or top of your list
It doesn't allow me to be full of joy or have a bit of sadness
Doing things for people, isn't what I like, it's what they wish
Remembering that death will be the one to deliver me my last
kiss
So don't blink, because you won't have a chance to see me
vanish

Wonder

There are so many questions unanswered, making us on the edge
Just like the disappearance of the letter x from this poetry book
Wondering if done by mistake or was it part of the agenda
Thinking that it wasn't to be known one way or another
Keeping the mystery closer to the back of the ledge
Knowing that it was the last place anyone would dare to look
Finding that only pursuing it would lead to total chaos or a plain fraud
Realizing the answers might not be what we want when they shall occur
If you wonder all the time, then you'll never know the truth
It is good to dream, but don't lose all aspects of your life
Even though most dreams are some form of your true history
Doesn't mean you can't wonder, just be in complete control of them
Remember when you thought that a leather seat was no different than a booth
Well it was until we decided to cut it open with a knife
Learning that nothing is what it seems unless you believe
So while others still have questions, you will take whatever will come
Not knowing if you will encounter them sooner or later
Deciding if it's all fake or not is all that you'll ever wonder

Wrath

Depression will only add fire to the flame of your wrath
Controlling it is something, you might be successful with
And in the other case, it will destroy all you have worked for
So ask yourself if you want to proceed, or just call it quits
Sure there is help for this kind of problem, but are you brave enough
Forgetting all you have learned, so you will be able to soak the knowledge
Craving it is one thing, but being forced into it is another
Getting rid of the garbage, clearing out your new path
Starting fresh, making your past sound like a total myth
Knowing that even though, it is worth it you will always be sore
Wondering why the harder you begin to push, the better it gets
Realizing how you were wrong for thinking that it was rough
No longer, having to live life on the edge
Not knowing if going to be loved, or surrounded by smother
Either way you won't care, as long as you're happy
Finding out that this choice was given out of good faith
And the advantages of this accomplishment is what you want to see
Being grateful to have this chance to get rid of the wrath

Write

An artist may draw, while a writer must write
Sure I can write short stories or essays but that ain't my style
Mine is very unique and consists of the talent I possess
Which is called poetry and is unlike any that have been seen
Even though many have read, none have experienced anything like this
Working hard trying to keep in competition from day to night
Knowing that I can write a poem faster than you can change that dial
You shouldn't be upset, but happy for my success
Don't worry if my words are complicated, because they are all clean
Please keep your eyes opened, because this is something you don't want to miss
Over the years I've been through many difficult times
Realizing that you'll have to live day to day not knowing what will happen
Because at any moment you can leave without a trace
That's what made me dedicate my life to the art of writing
Now I'm happy because I get to work with many different rhymes
Thinking of the many doors that it has and will open
Not worrying if I'll get out of step, as long as I keep in pace
Believing that this is a lot better than always fighting

Yield

You begin to ask yourself if you had the right of way
Would you be nice and give it up, just to yield
Or do you take it without any hesitation or regret
Either way you decide, put yourself in their shoes
If you think about it, then you will come up with the best decision
Knowing that once made, you have to stick with your emotions
Because you have no one but yourself to point the blame toward
So what if yesterday is ruined, at least you'll make it up today
Remembering that your heart and soul is something nobody can steal
Putting everything into perspective, making sure the day has been set
Realizing that whatever the future brings, nobody ever knows
Running into déjà vu like never before, causing a terrible collision
Hopefully you will remember this, and stop taking notations
The sooner you learn, the better you will be able to move forward
Not judging a book by its cover, but by what's inside
Sorting out all the stories that have become, to find what is real
Telling the truth instead of taking them for that unwanted ride
Feeling that you should be the last person they expect to yield

Zero

Instead of me treating you as a ten, you think of me as a zero
Not knowing what I did exactly for this treatment
Whatever it is, I am glad it happened and do it again
If all I'm good for, is someone that you can walk all over
Then forget you, because I deserve better than that
I think that I have earned at least more respect than a dead pharaoh
Knowing that you will get yours on the Day of Judgment
Wondering why in the world, I did everything I can
Watching it pass my eyes as I looked into the future
Staring and seeing for the third time, that same black cat
If you think that I'm anything like you, you're wrong
I'm nothing like any of you, I'm very unique and different
I see things more clearly and openly than the majority
Feeling things you wouldn't possibly begin to understand
Realizing that being with you, I will never belong
Sure I'm used to being alone, because I'm very independent
But don't give me any of your sorrow or pity
Because forgiveness is something I won't allow you to demand